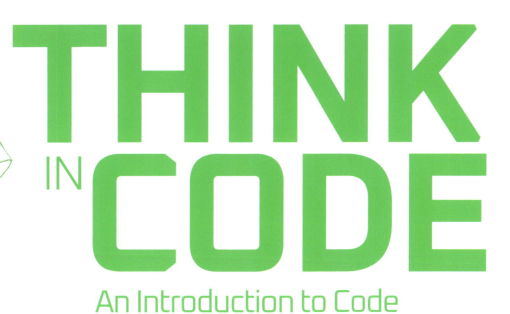

THINK
IN CODE

An Introduction to Code

Written and Illustrated by
Marcus J. Carey

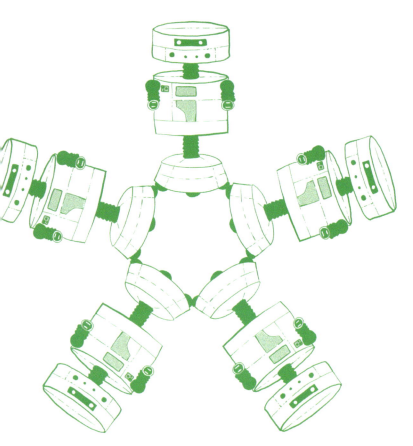
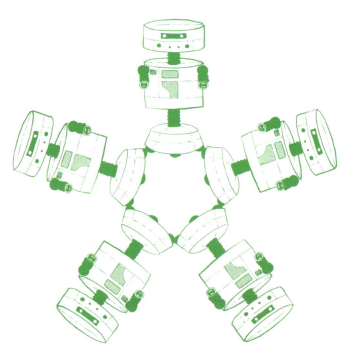

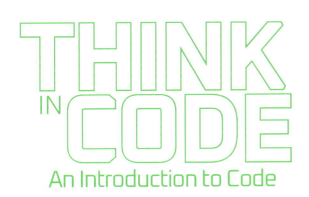

THINK IN CODE
An Introduction to Code

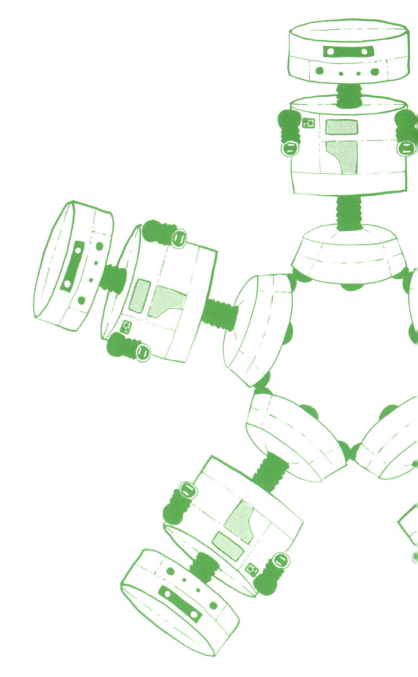

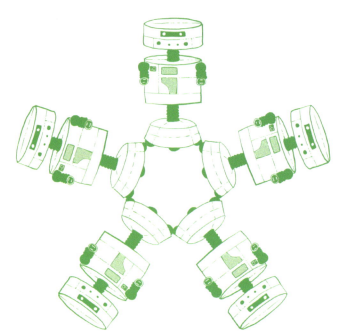

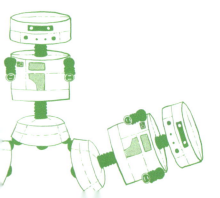

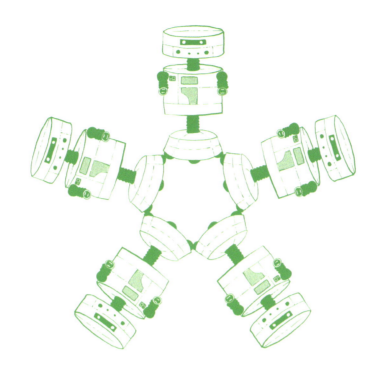

This book is dedicated to my wife, children, and grandkids.

You all continue to inspire me.

I love you all.

-MJC

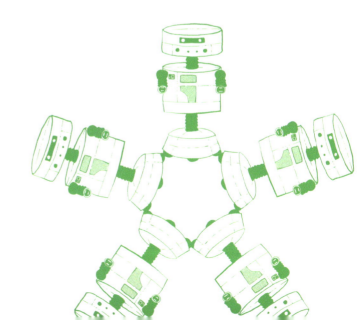

BEGIN

Get ready to train a robot.

In order to train a robot, you have to understand how they learn.

To get started you'll need your imagination.

You are going to have to use your brain to think in code.

Robots are powered by computers.

Just like any other computer device such as smart phones or tablets your robot uses code and memory to store data.

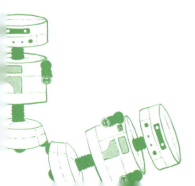

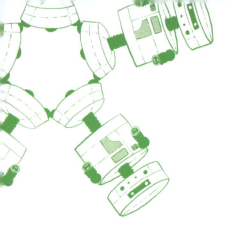

Data can be names, numbers, phone numbers or anything else you have your robot store.

To make data easy to retrieve, the robot's code stores them as variables.

A variable is like a magical box that can hold anything such as letters, numbers, words, and more.

This robot's code places a dollar sign in front of the variables.

For example the robot stores a name as `$name`.

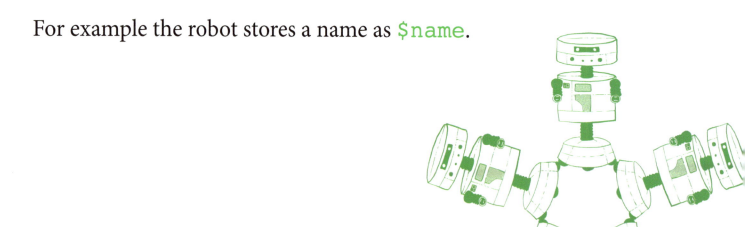

$name = "Alice"

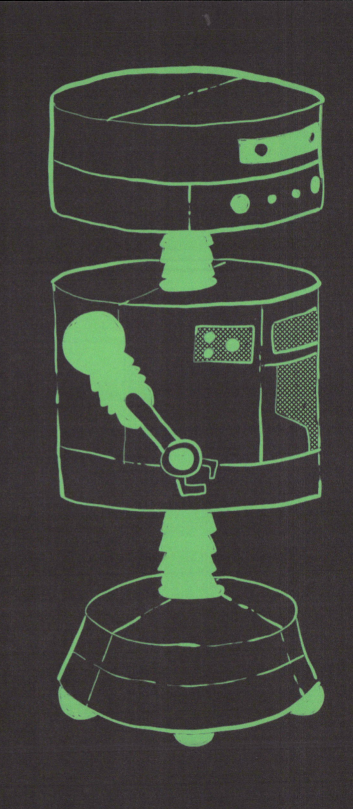

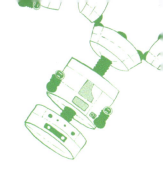

You are going to work with the robot so it can interact with humans.

Since this is an imaginary robot, you'll have to remember the variables and speak for it.

When you see quotes, please use your best robot voice as you are attempting to sound like a robot.

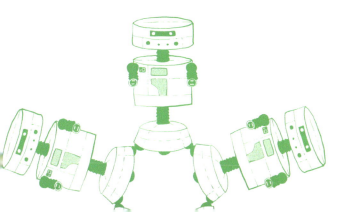

"What is your name?"

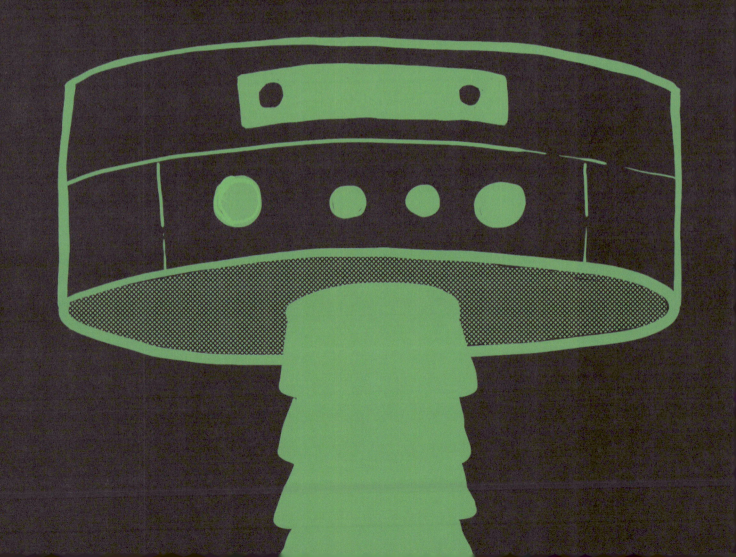

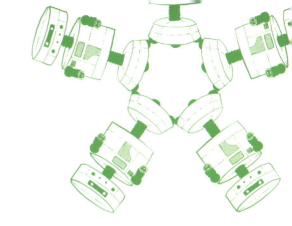

The robot saved your name as $name.

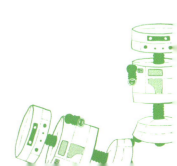

"What is your favorite food?"

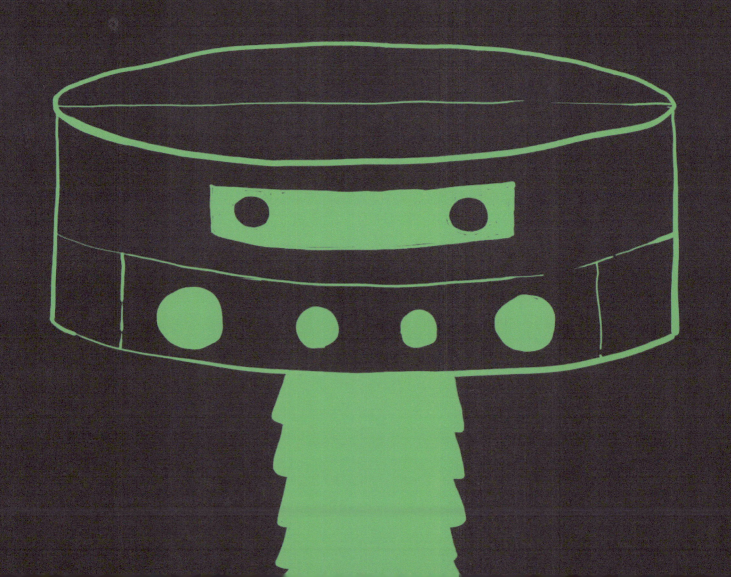

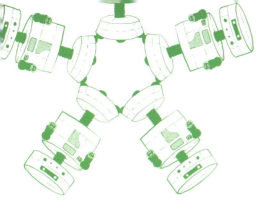

The robot saved your favorite food as `$food`.

"How old are you?"

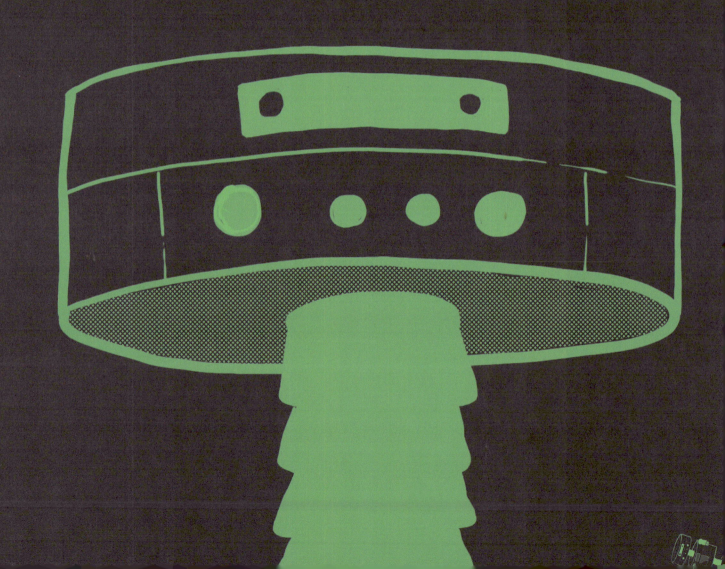

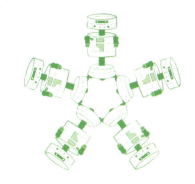

The robot saved your age as $age.

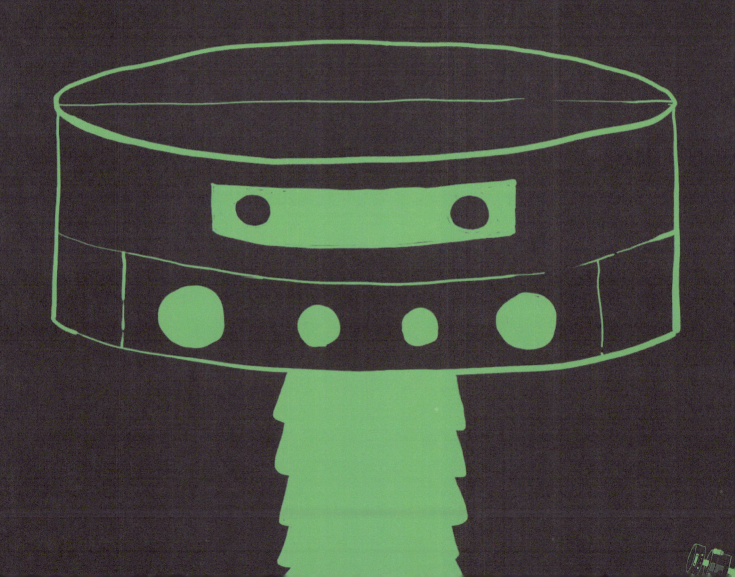

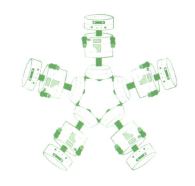

The robot saved your favorite color as $color.

Robots can also use code to do math with variables.

As you can see your robot created a variable named `$new_age`.

$new_age = $age + 1

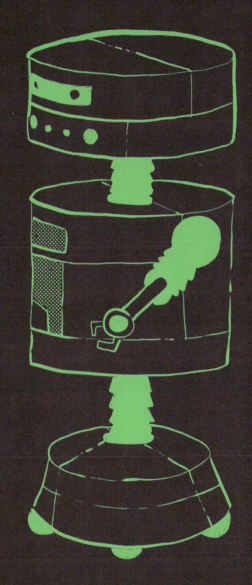

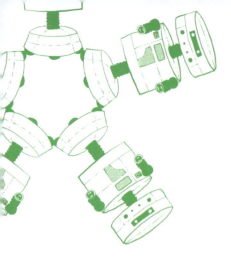

Now that your robot knows a few things about you, it can speak.

Well, you're going have to use your best robot voice to speak for it.

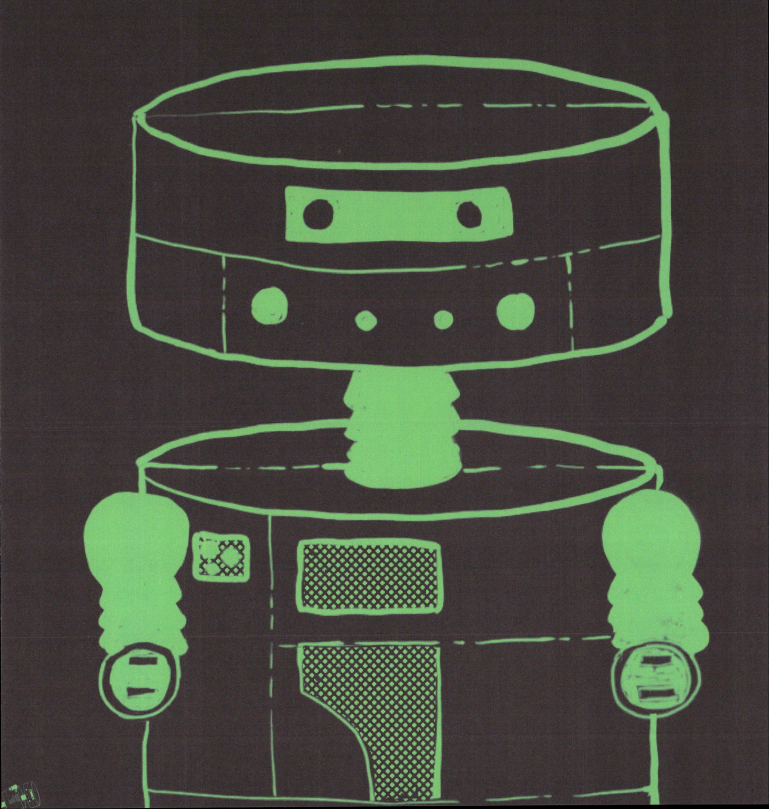

"Hello $name, how are you doing today?"

"You are currently $age years old."

"Next year you will be $new_age."

"On your birthday I will make sure you get $food."

"I'd love to paint your room $color."

"$name, thanks for speaking for me and helping me remember everything!"

Robots can also keep track of things with lists.

Lists can be kept in variables as well.

You can refer to items in the list by their index number.

Here is a list of animals.

`$animals = ["lions", "tigers", "bears"]`

The first index is `0`.

The index of `$animals[1]` value is `tigers`.

Use your robot voice to speak for the robot on the right.

"Hello $name."

"Are you afraid of animals[0], $animals[1], and $animals[2]?"

Robots can also remember things by mapping data with key and value pairs.

This can come in handy when a robot needs to speak different languages.

For example create a variable named `$spanish`.

You can use it to translate from English to Spanish by setting up keys and values.

```
$spanish["hello"] = "hola"
$spanish["one"] = "uno"
$spanish["two"] = "dos"
$spanish["three"] = "tres"
```

So the key `$spanish["two"]` value is `dos`.

Use your robot voice to speak for the robot on the right.

"$spanish["hello"] $name!"

"I can count backwards in Spanish!"

"$spanish["three"]!"

"$spanish["two"]!"

"$spanish["one"]!"

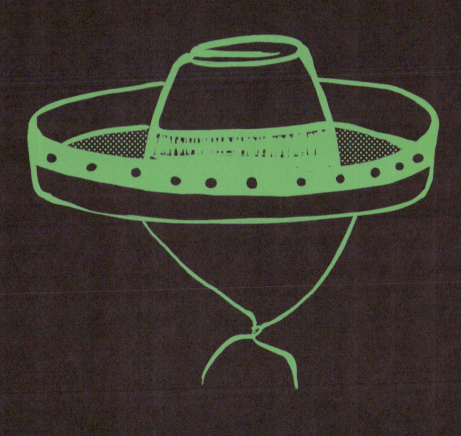

Now you need to understand the basic math the robot needs to operate.

In code you will often count up and down to accomplish tasks.

This simple math is called incrementing and decrementing.

Incrementing is increasing the value of variables.

Decrementing is decreasing the value of variables.

You saw incrementing earlier when the robot did the `$new_age = $age + 1` calculation.

"$spanish["hello"] $name!"

"I can count backwards in Spanish!"

"$spanish["three"]!"

"$spanish["two"]!"

"$spanish["one"]!"

Now you need to understand the basic math the robot needs to operate.

In code you will often count up and down to accomplish tasks.

This simple math is called incrementing and decrementing.

Incrementing is increasing the value of variables.

Decrementing is decreasing the value of variables.

You saw incrementing earlier when the robot did the `$new_age = $age + 1` calculation.

Now you'll teach the robot how to be a baseball umpire.

The game of baseball is easy for the robot to learn because it uses a lot of incrementing.

The robot needs to understand two conditions for now:

   1. If the batter gets four balls they get a walk to first base.
   2. If the batter gets three strikes they are out.

The robot starts with the two variables to the right.

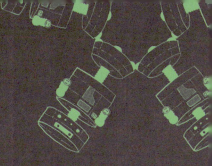

$strikes = 0
$balls = 0

The code that the robot would run would be similar to the logic on the right.

The robot would evaluate the conditions for each batter.

You are using `if` conditions which allows the robot make decisions.

Now you have to pretend to be a robot again and run this code.

Pick strikes or balls to evaluate the `if` conditions.

You may flip a coin if you'd like to add a more random picker.

As the values increment the batter will strike out or walk to first base.

```
if pitch is a strike?
    $strikes = $strikes + 1

if $strikes is equal to 3?
    batter strikes out
    set $strikes & $balls to 0

if pitch is a ball?
    $balls = $balls + 1

if $balls is equal to 4?
    batter walks to first base
    set $strikes & $balls to 0
```

You are now training the robot to launch rockets into space.

Since decrementing is the opposite of incrementing you will be counting down to a certain number.

You need to create a timer variable for ten seconds.

`$timer = 10`

You can use fingers or other objects to keep track of `$timer` value.

Use the conditions on the right here.

Decrement `$timer` after you evaluate the conditions, then repeat the `if` conditions until the rocket takes off.

```
if $timer not equal 0
   $timer = $timer - 1


if $timer equals 0
   rocket takes off


$timer = timer - 1
```
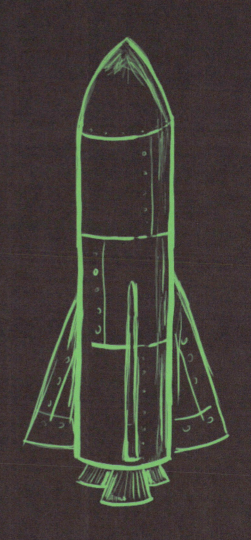

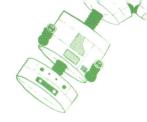

Congratulations!

You used your mind to think in code to accomplish tasks.

Just as you helped the imaginary robot perform tasks, humans rely on computers and robots to perform complex tasks every day.

They perform tasks based on what their code instructs them to do.

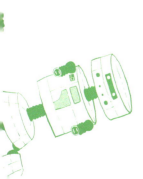

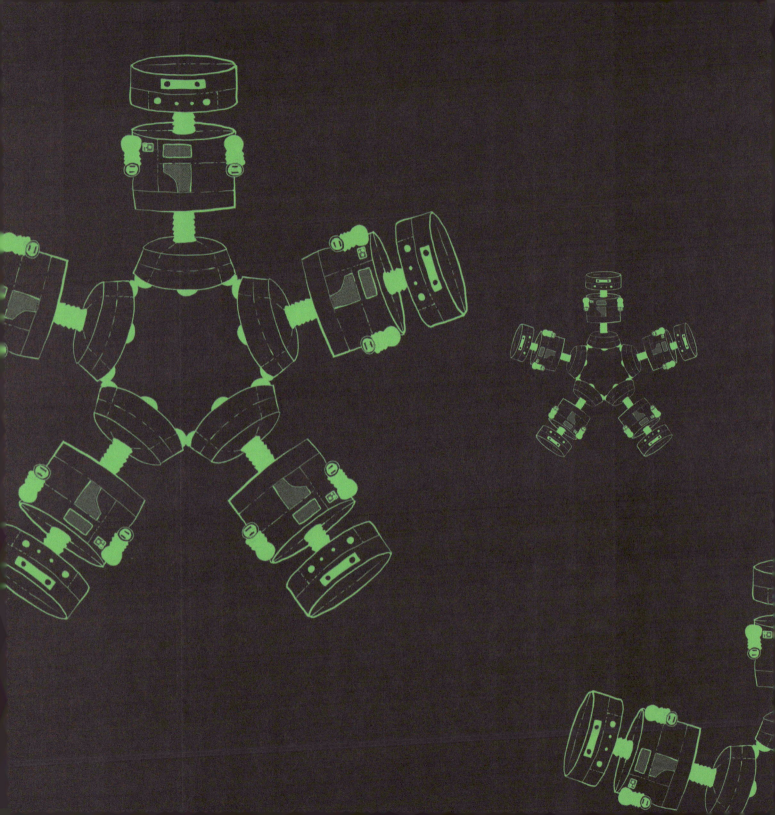

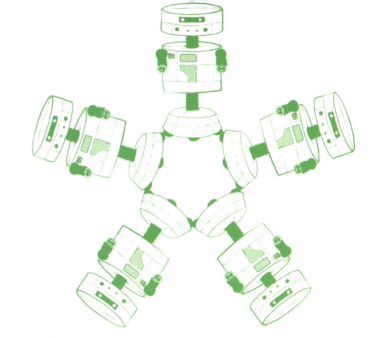

You can create code that help cure the sick.

You can make code that help feed the hungry.

You can build code to help humans go to Mars.

With code you are only limited by your imagination.

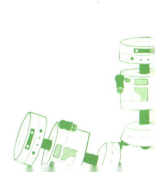

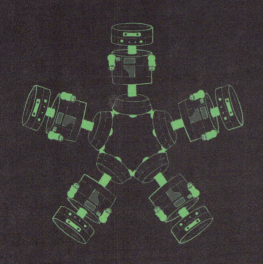

END

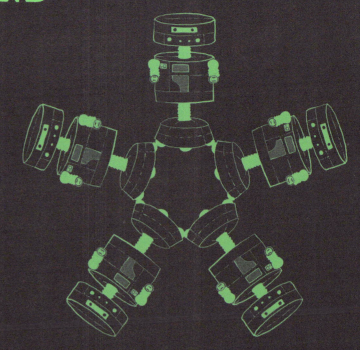

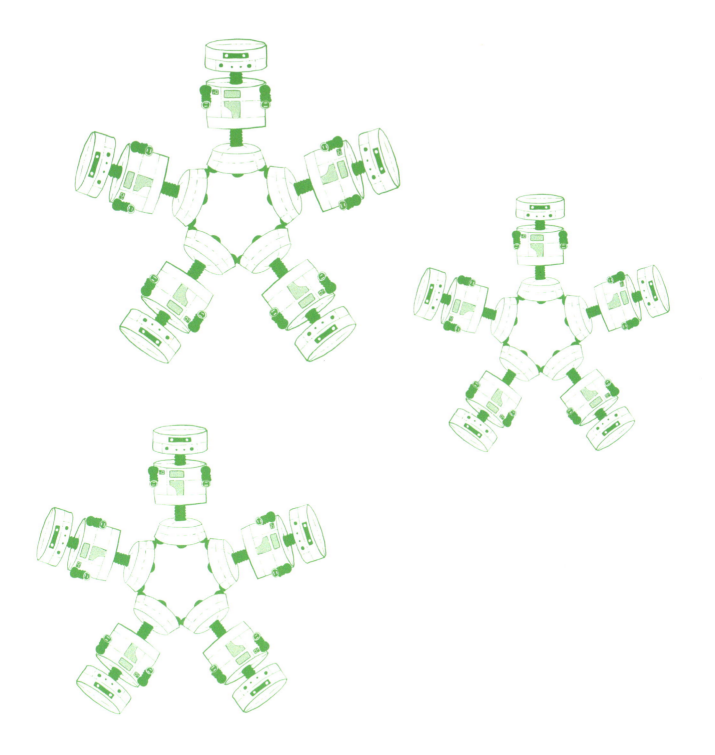

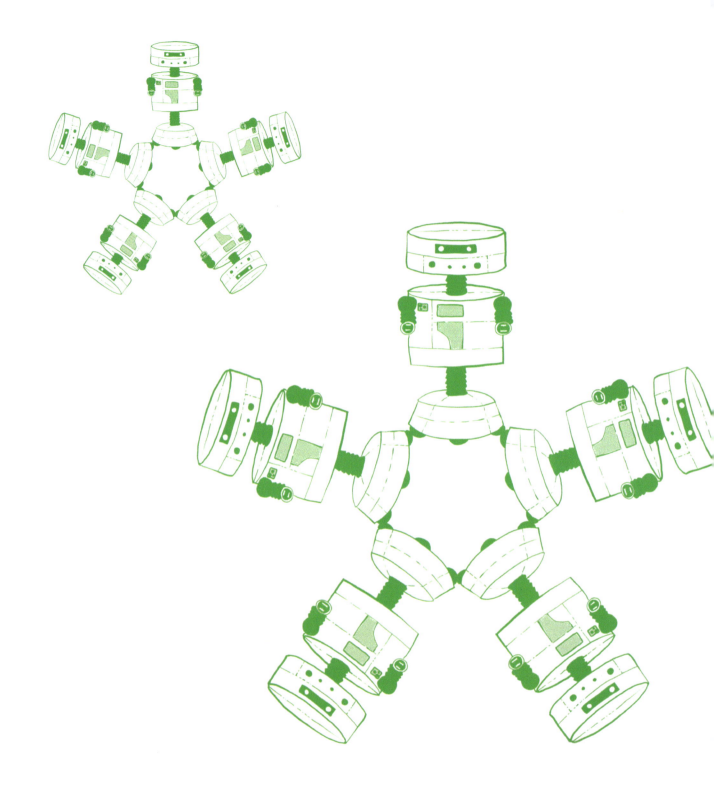